Pirates
and their Lost Treasures

An Informative Guide For
Treasure Hunters!

Pirates
and their Lost Treasures

An Informative Guide For Treasure Hunters!

**by
T&S Publications**

© 2023 T&S Publications
Cedar Key, Fl. 32625
ISBN: 978-1-7360054-7-7
Library of Congress Control Number: 2023901789
All Rights Reserved.

No part of this book may be copied or reproduced in any form or by any means without the express written consent of the copyright owner. For personal use only.

Every effort has been made to ensure the accuracy of the information presented however this book is issued with the understanding that no liability will be accepted for any loss or profit, direct or otherwise as a consequence of using this information.

DISCLAIMER

T&S Publications assumes NO liability for any misfortune of any kind concerning treasure hunting or any associated or non-associated activities. We recommend following safety procedures and using common sense at ALL times.

Made in the United States.

Table of Contents:

Introduction..7
Captain William Kidd...................................9
Henry Every (Avery)...................................21
Blackbeard...29
Calico Jack..39
Sir Francis Drake.......................................47
Olivier Levasseur.......................................59
Amaro Pargo...69
Spanish Treasure Fleet (1715)....................77
Jean Lafitte—Wild Card..............................85
José Gaspar—Real or Myth........................99

and More:

Gasparilla Pirate Festival..........................101
Popular Pirate Festivals............................102
Treasure Hunting Quick Tips....................105
Treasure Hunting Log Book......................106
Glossary..107
Research and Resources..........................112
A Note to Treasure Hunters......................115
T&S Publications.....................................116

Introduction

This book was written to provide useful information to those interested in "pirate treasure".

At the time of this writing, the pirates featured all have lost treasures... or what we suspect are lost treasures that could be worth millions today.

So, we have arranged this book accordingly. First, a brief description of the pirate is given, then right to the good stuff... the treasure (lol)! Giving the reader a few options (both popular and in some cases bizarre) as to the treasures possible whereabouts, then a more in-depth look at the pirates life. We believe that where the pirate frequently visited in his travels could also be a clue.

Honestly, if we knew where "X marks the spot" was, we would be digging it up ourselves... because we are treasure hunters.

In conclusion, we hope to provide a "credible" and "valid" source of information as to the pirates themselves and their lost treasures. All the best!!

We hope you enjoy our book,

Pirates and their Lost Treasures.

Sincerely,

T&S Publications

1. Captain William Kidd
(1645 – 1701)

Captain Kidd on Gardiner's Island with his treasure by Howard Pyle, published in Harper's New Monthly Magazine, 1894.

William Kidd, also known as Captain Kidd, was a Scottish sea captain who was commissioned as a privateer but was convicted as a pirate. He sailed in the Atlantic, Caribbean and Indian oceans.

- **Captain Kidd's Lost Treasure:** Knowing he was wanted as a pirate, Capt. Kidd returned to Boston to clear his name but took precautions. He buried treasure on Gardiner's Island (New York), which was found to contain a chest and box of gold, gold dust, box of silver, silver bars, Spanish dollars, rubies, diamonds, porringers (small bowls) and candlesticks. There was over one thousand ounces of gold alone which is currently well over a million dollars.

Capt. William Kidd's inventory 1699: A receipt was given to Jonathan Gardiner for Captain Kidd's treasure dug up on Gardiner's Island (7/25/1699). Document can be found at the **East Hampton Library, Long Island Collection.**

Having been tricked and put in the Boston gaol (jail), Kidd sent word of a deal for the Governor that if he were to be set free, he would retrieve a <u>large treasure</u> left in the Caribbean. The deal was not accepted and **that treasure has not yet been recovered.**

- **Possible locations for his treasure are:**
  1. Caribbean - The *Quedagh Merchant,* an Indian vessel captured and renamed the *Adventure Prize,* was used by Capt. Kidd, and found in December of 2007 in the shallow waters of the Dominican Republic. Though it had been stripped, abandoned and scuttled (sunk), Capt. Kidd was in this area prior to returning to Boston. He was also in Madagascar.

  2. Block Island (About 9 miles off the mainland of Rhode Island) – A place that Captain Kidd had visited and received food and hospitality from a Mrs. Mercy Raymond. Capt. Kidd was said to have asked her to hold out her apron then he filled it with gold and jewels as payment for her kindness.

  3. Various places around New Jersey such as Cape May and Sandy Hook, also Cliffwood beach, west of Long Island, New York. These places have stories and legends attached to Captain Kidd's buried treasure.

  4. Grand Manan (a Canadian Island) – It is thought that treasure was possibly buried there by Capt. Kidd while he was a privateer.

  5. One theory exists about Kidd's treasure having been found and dug up on an Island off communist Vietnam but because of the danger it was buried again. The person has since passed away however there is still a detailed article that can be read about this claim. See *"Further Research" at the end of this chapter.*

6. Palmer-Kidd Charts – In the late 1920's, Hubert and Guy Palmer (brothers) who were knowledgeable collectors of pirate artifacts claimed they had found old sea charts hidden in secret compartments of furniture that belonged to Captain Kidd. Four items were reportedly found in several chests and a bureau which were on parchment (yellow and aged). The parchment seemed to be from the right time period. These items have an island drawn with possible instructions and an "X" along with "China Sea" written on them.

7. Oak Island, Nova Scotia, has long been a possible candidate for Capt. Kidd's treasure. The "Money Pit" on the Island appears to be a complex flooding trap and items found such as scraps of parchment paper tested by radiocarbon dating are consistent with the 16th century.

William Kidd, 18th century portrait by Sir James Thornhill. (public domain)

Early Life

William Kidd, also known as Captain Kidd, was possibly born in Greenock, Scotland in 1645 however there have been claims that his birthplace was Dundee, Scotland. Little is known about his youth but it is believed he went to sea during this time.

Privateer/Pirate

In 1689, Kidd was a crew member for a French Captain named Jean Fantin. Kidd and the crew mutinied and commandeered the ship, sailing it to the English colony of Nevis (Island). Kidd became the Captain and the ship was renamed the *Blessed William*.

England was now at war with the French, (the Nine Years War) and Captain Kidd was loyal to England (the British Crown). The Governor of Nevis, Christopher Codrington, assembled a small fleet to defend the island from the French and the *Blessed William* joined. The Governor may have encouraged Kidd to get his pay from the French.

Kidd and his men then attacked the French Island of Marie-Galante, they destroyed and looted it collecting an estimated 2000 pounds sterling.

Now battling against French warships, Captain Kidd's crew did not agree with his decisions and turned against him. Led by crew member and pirate Robert Culliford, they stole his ship and left him stranded.

Despite this set back, Kidd returned to New York and was hired and financed as a privateer. He captured an enemy privateer ship off the New England coast and was also rewarded 150 pounds for privateer work in the Caribbean.

While in New York, William Kidd had gotten married to a wealthy widow.

Personal Life

On May 16, 1691, William Kidd married Sarah Kidd (Sarah Bradley Cox Oort – maiden name Bradley, 21 years old) in New York.

Sarah was twice the widow and very wealthy. Her second husband had died just two days before Sarah applied for a marriage license to wed William Kidd. After the expedited wedding, they moved into a mansion on Pearl Street in New York. Records indicate they had 2 children.

Kidd was also active in the building of the Trinity Church and owned a church pew.

Privateer/Pirate

In 1695, Kidd was asked by Lord Bellomont (Richard Coote), the new Governor of New York to privateer and attack the pirates along with any enemy French ships. The request was backed by the British Crown and a group of Nobles, so refusal would have been considered to be "disloyal."

Kidd returned to England and received a *letter of marque,* signed by the King, which gave Kidd the authority to seize and recover all "booty" with the profits being divided and a portion going to the British Crown.

In 1696, Captain Kidd was placed in command of the *Adventure Galley,* an over 284 ton hybrid ship with both sails and oars, 34 cannons and approximately 150 men.

While the Adventure Galley sailed down the Thames River, it passed by a British Naval frigate which Kidd failed to salute. This offended the Naval Commander, who then pressed (took) much of his crew for naval service. Now seriously shorthanded, Kidd sailed to New York to add more crew members however some that joined were pirates or criminals themselves.

Now with an increased crew, Kidd weighed anchor and set sail for the Cape of Good Hope near South Africa. Unfortunately, due to a sudden epidemic and illness, Kidd lost at least a third of his crew. His ship was also leaking.

A ship Captain of the British East India Company reported that Kidd had tried to attack a Mughal (India) convoy being escorted but he was run off.

Though Kidd refused to attack certain ships because they were "out of bounds" according to his commission, the situation was turning desperate.

In 1697, Kidd killed one of his crew, his gunner William Moore. The crew was rebellious and an argument followed then Kidd struck Moore in the head with a heavy bucket and he died the next day.

As things became increasingly desperate, Kidd turned to piracy. By using the trick of flying French colors (flag) he was able to capture a Dutch owned ship that produced a "French Pass" which at least gave Kidd some legal justification for his actions however the rewards were little.

After some failed attempts, finally in 1698, Kidd raised French colors (flag) and approached the 400-ton *Quedagh Merchant,* a vessel loaded with gold, silver, gems, silks and East Indian merchandise bound for India. Though the ship had French colors, it's Captain was an Englishman who had purchased protection from the French Crown. Kidd tried to persuade his crew to stop but they refused claiming the ship had French Passes which counted as French. Kidd succumbed to his crew and kept the French passes (possibly for a defense) and the *Quedagh*

Merchant. He released it's crew and renamed the ship the *Adventure Prize,* then set sail for Madagascar.

News of Kidd's acts of piracy were reported to the British Crown which resulted in a circular letter sent out to arrest Kidd and his crew.

Upon Kidd's arrival in Madagascar, long time foe and pirate Robert Culliford was there with his ship the *Mocha Frigate*. Kidd claimed he gave orders to his crew to attack Culliford's ship but the crew refused. Some of Kidd's crew abandoned him and joined Culliford.

From there, Kidd decided to head for the Caribbean, however the *Adventure Galley* was leaking and in bad shape so he left it behind and ordered it burnt. Now, with the remainder of his crew, he sailed to the Caribbean in the *Adventure Prize* (formerly the *Quedagh Merchant)*.

After reaching the Caribbean, he knew the Adventure Prize was a marked vessel. He sold the plunder and hid the ship leaving it anchored in a lagoon and hired merchants to guard it for a few months. He and some of his crew then sailed for New England in a small sloop to clear his name.

Trial and Death

Knowing the danger that was waiting for him, Kidd buried treasure on Gardiner's Island to use as a "bargaining chip" then sailed around the eastern tip of Long Island and doubled back.

Kidd sent a message to Lord Bellomont saying he was ready to negotiate a pardon and he believed he had rightly acted according to his Royal Commission. Lord Bellomont however feared being criminally implicated himself and set a trap for Kidd. Bellomont lured Kidd to Boston with false promises and had him arrested. Kidd was placed in the Boston goal (jail), in harsh conditions for over a year before being sent to England. Kidd's wife was also arrested. Though it is unknown how long Kidd's wife was in jail, it is believed that there was a "lack of evidence" to keep her in jail.

While waiting trial in England, he wrote to the King several times requesting clemency but the atmosphere had changed and was against him.

Defending himself against the charges of the murder of William Moore and piracy, the evidence he had handed over to Bellomont's lawyer, a statement and the "French passes" were now missing.

Kidd was found guilty on all charges and sentenced to be hanged in public on May 23rd 1701. On the first attempt, the hangman's rope broke and Kidd survived. Some of the people felt that was an act of God and called for his release, however he was hanged again minutes later and died.

His body was covered with tar and left hanging over the Thames River at Tilbury Point (England) for over two years, as a warning to others.

Hanging of William Kidd from The Pirates Own Book by Charles Ellms– 1837 (public domain)

Further Research

There is a detailed article at this on-line newspaper, Daily Mail (.com) that talks about a man named Richard Knight, who claimed he dug up Captain Kidd's treasure and figured it was worth about 40 million. Found on the Vietnam Island of Hon Tre Lon, Mr. Knight dug it up and said it was so dangerous that he reburied the "booty" on another island (west coast of Thailand). Mr. Knight was arrested and spent over a year in jail. He has since passed away.

More can be read at this website: https://www.dailymail.co.uk/news/article-2235400/Did-Sussex-bounty-hunter-dig-Captain-Kidds-treasure-Hunt-12m-haul-gold-coins

2. Henry Every (Avery)
King of the Pirates
(Uncertain, 1653 -1665 – Uncertain, 1699 –1714)

Pirate Captain Henry Every with his ship the "Fancy" in the background. (public domain)

Henry Every (or Avery), also known by other names such as John Avery, Long Ben or King of the Pirates, was an English Pirate who operated in the Atlantic and Indian oceans, turning to piracy at about 1691 and continuing till 1696. He eluded capture and disappeared.

- **Henry Every's Lost Treasure:**
  Every raided and looted a massive treasure ship in 1695 belonging to India's Grand Mughal (Emperor Aurangzeb), the *Ganj-i-Sawai*. Every stole gold and precious jewels, what was possibly as much as 600,000 British pounds worth (equivalent to tens of millions today). It is believed to be one of the **richest ships ever taken by pirates.**

India's Grand Mughal, Emperor Aurangzeb, painting by an unknown artist, 18th century.
(public domain)

- **Coins Found:** In 2014, a treasure hunter found an Arabian coin with a metal detector dated 1693 and minted in Yemen (western Asia), in an orchard in Rhode Island.

  More coins were found by other treasure hunters... ten in Massachusetts, three in Rhode Island and two in Connecticut. These coins suggest that some of Every's crew may have been able to settle in New England (US) at the time and integrate however not enough evidence exists for a definite conclusion.

- **Possible locations for his treasure are:**

  1. There was a hand written note that was thought to be by Every to a trusted friend that had the details of three chests containing large rubies, sapphires, emeralds, topazes, diamonds, 25 gold bars and various pieces of gold that he buried in the cliffs near Lizard Point in Southern Cornwall, England (UK). *For more information, see "**Hand Written Note**" near the end of this chapter.*

  <u>What happened to Henry Every?</u>

  2. Some claim that Every had changed his name, boarded a sloop and returned to England where he retired.

  3. Another claim said that he returned to

England but had lost his fortune, died in great poverty and was buried near a Bideford church.

According to the book, **"A General History of the Pyrates"** (Their first Rise and Settlement in the Island of Providence to the present Time) written in 1724, it says, "he traveled on foot to Biddiford... he fell sick and died; not being worth as much as would buy him a coffin."

4. Still another claim is that he returned to live on a tropical island under an alias name. See *"**Further Research**" at the end of this chapter.*

Every was legendary for successfully escaping with his treasure without being arrested or killed in battle. **After 1696, it is not clear as to what happened to Henry Every. <u>His treasure has not yet been recovered.</u>**

Early Life
Henry Every, was believed to be born around 1653 (or as late as 1665) near Plymouth, Devon, England. Records suggest that he was the son of John and Anne Every.

Personal Life
According to a confession by William Phillips, a member of his crew, he was "aged about 40 years," his mother lived "near Plymouth," and his wife was a periwig seller who lived "in Ratcliffe Highway" (London). Records suggest that he was

married in London in September of 1690. There is no evidence that he had any children.

It is believed that "Henry Every" was his real name because he used this name when he entered the Royal Navy.

Royal Navy

Probably a sailor from youth, Every's service in the Royal Navy may have been from 1671 to 1690. Accounts of him having served as a Midshipmen, a Buccaneer and a Master's Mate collaborate with this record. In August of 1690, he was discharged from the Royal Navy.

Atlantic Slave Trade

A few years after his discharge, Every was suspected of illegally selling slaves without a license. One report said he would lure slave traders on to his ship by flying friendly English colors (flag) then seized them and carried them away.

Spanish Expedition Shipping

Several investors from London assembled a fleet for a venture called the Spanish Expedition Shipping. It was four warships: the *Seventh Son, Dove, James* and the *Charles II*. Their mission was to conduct trade, recover treasure and attack French vessels in the West Indies.

Every joined and quickly was promoted to first mate of the *Charles II*, a 46-gun privateer ship. While in the city of La Coruna (Spain), after the crew had "no pay" for months, Every led the crew in a mutiny.

Pirate Life

Every quickly renamed the ship, the *Charles II* to the *Fancy*. He sailed to Madagascar, robbing and looting for supplies and adding to his crew.

Now with about 150 men in his crew, he stopped at the Island of Johanna (in the Indian ocean) and cleverly wrote a letter to the English ship commanders falsely saying he had not attacked any English ships. This was thought to be a trick to keep the English from pursuing him however it didn't work.

Every then headed for the Red Sea where he joined forces with other pirate captains such as Thomas Tew, Joseph Faro, William Want, Thomas Wake and William May.

In 1695, an Indian convoy, which Every knew would be passing by, consisted of about 25 ships including the massive treasure ship *Ganj-i-sawai* and its escort, the *Fath Mahmamadi*. The convoy briefly eluded the pirates during the night but the pirates soon caught up. They attacked and plundered the *Fath Mahmamadi* first, which had an estimated treasure of 60,000 British pounds. They then attacked the *Ganj-i-sawai*, which lost it's mainmast in battle and was unable to escape. There was a hand-to-hand combat but the pirates won and plundered that treasure, estimated to be possibly as much as 600,000 British pounds worth.

There were reports that the pirates horribly brutalized the captives for days afterwards, with some women even committing suicide.

Pirate Captain Thomas Tew and some of the pirate crew had been killed. After dividing up the treasure and gems, the pirate fleet split up and went their separate ways.

Though Every and his crew were now rich, they were also marked men. The attack on Emperor Aurangzeb's treasure ship plus the poor treatment of the women had serious consequences for England. India shut down factories who dealt with the English, arrested the English subjects and valuable English trade agreements were nearing cancellation. A bounty of 1,000 pounds was put on Every's head and he was now the focus of a worldwide manhunt.

Every set sail for the West Indies, however not all of his crew wanted to go so he purchased slaves for the long journey. After finally reaching New Providence (Bahamas), Every used an alias name and successfully bought protection for him and his crew from the Island's Governor Nicholas Trott.

Soon however, the proclamation to apprehend Every and his crew reached Governor Trott. He denied knowing who Every was but did alert the authorities as to his whereabouts.

After that, Every was said to have tried to buy a pardon from the Governor of Jamaica (William Beaston) who refused his offer.

The pirates split up with reports of some staying in the West Indies, some going to the American colonies and some to parts unknown.

The last record of Henry Every was in 1696. Though the manhunt for Every continued long afterwards and sightings were often reported, no reliable information had emerged.

Hand Written Note

As to the claim of the hand written note from Every to a trusted friend concerning his buried treasure in England (mentioned in the beginning of this chapter). Two business men who believed this claim, was said to have conducted a treasure hunt in 1779 for two years but the hunt ended when a descendant of Every told them he had died a pauper (poor).

Further Research

There is an interesting article in "The Saba Islander" written by Will Johnson and entitled "Henry Every *alias* John Avery." Mr. Johnson gives a detailed article in which Henry Every may have been living on Saba under the alias of John Avery (and had a family). A significant piece of information he states concerns a Population List for the island of Saba taken in 1728.

Saba is a small Caribbean island in the Lesser Antilles chain.

More information can be found at this website: https://thesabaislander.com/2018/10/04/henry-every-alias-john-avery

3. Blackbeard

(approx. 1680 – 1718)

Pirate Captain Edward Teach (Blackbeard) during the "Golden Age of Piracy." (public domain)

Edward Teach was an English Pirate, better known as Blackbeard, who operated around the West Indies and the eastern coast of North America between 1716–1718.

- **Blackbeard's Lost Treasure:** Blackbeard's flagship, the *Queen Anne's Revenge,* was found with many artifacts but no "pirate's treasure". Speculated to be in the millions, his treasure **has not yet been recovered.**

- **Possible locations for his treasure are:**

Map of Ocracoke Inlet, N.C. in 1775.
(public domain)

1. The place of Blackbeard's final battle, Ocracoke Island, North Carolina. Now, it is a tourist hot-spot that can be reached by ferry.

2. Topsail Island, N.C., is believed by some to be where Blackbeard hid his treasure before his final battle. The Island is accessible by car but driving on the beach has restrictions. Currently, metal detecting is allowed on the beach however any items over 100 years old fall under archaeological laws.

3. Plum Point in Bath, North Carolina where Blackbeard had his home for a short while.

4. Archbell Point, North Carolina where Governor Charles Eden and his secretary Tobias Knight lived. Gov. Eden granted Blackbeard a pardon and was suspected of possibly conspiring with him.

5. The Caribbean. Blackbeard was known to have attacked ships throughout the Caribbean and had been near the islands of Martinique, St. Vincent, the Grenadines, the Bahamas and more.

Appearance

Edward Teach (Blackbeard) was described as having a thick black beard he wore very long and sometimes braided. A tall man with broad shoulders who wore knee-length boots and dark clothing, topped with a wide hat. In times of battle, he was said to have worn a sling over his shoulders with pistols hanging in holsters and a cutlass (a short broad slashing sword).

Teach was said to be a very shrewd and clever man. He often relied on his intimidating image instead of the use of violence on the victims he robbed.

Early Life

Blackbeard was presumably born in Bristol, Kingdom of England around 1680. Although he was also known as Edward Teach or Edward Thatch, the use of fictitious names were commonly used by pirates as a way to protect their family name. It is possible that these may not be his real name.

Much is unknown about his early life but it is believed that because he was most likely raised in what was then the second-largest city in England, that he could almost certainly read and write.

Before Blackbeard's life as a pirate, the 18th-century author Charles Johnson claimed that Edward Teach was a sailor on privateer ships in Jamaica during the War of the Spanish Succession.

Pirate Life

Possibly around 1716, Teach joined the crew of Captain Benjamin Hornigold, a renowned pirate that operated in the waters of New Providence (what is now the Bahamas).

Soon, Hornigold placed Teach in charge of his

own sloop (sailboat). Early in 1717, Hornigold and Teach, each captaining a sloop, set a course for the mainland.

During this alliance, the pirates attacked and plundered merchant ships taking the valuables, food, liquor, weapons and cargo. They also commandeered two more sloops.

Hornigold then decided to accept the King's pardon offered by the British government to former privateers and he retired.

At that time, Hornigold took the sloop named *Ranger* and one other sloop leaving Teach on the sloop named *Revenge* with the remaining sloop. They parted ways with reports that they never met up again.

In November of 1717, Teach's two ships attacked a French merchant ship carrying a cargo of slaves called the *La Concorde*. He commandeered the larger vessel then sailed south along *St Vincent and the Grenadines* where they disembarked the crew of the *La Concorde* and also gave them the two smaller sloops.

He then renamed the ship *La Concorde* to *Queen Anne's Revenge* and equipped her with 40 guns.

In December of 1717, Teach had stopped a merchant sloop named the *Margaret,* the Captain and crew were held as prisoners aboard the *Queen Anne's Revenge* for about eight hours and were forced to watch their own sloop ransacked. Afterwards, Teach allowed them to leave on the *Margaret* unharmed. The Captain later reported the matter and detailed that Teach was in command of two vessels and at least 300 men.

Other later reports included a third ship also.

In March of 1718, another pirate named David Herriot and his crew were invited to join the pirates and they accepted the invitation. Herriot's sloop the *Adventure* was now included and as they sailed for the Bay of Honduras, another ship and 4 more sloops were also added.

In April of 1718, Teach's enlarged fleet looted, burned and attacked other vessels as they made their way up the eastern coast of Florida heading for Charles Town (currently called Charleston), in the Province of South Carolina.

Blockade of Charles Town

In May of 1718, Teach was at his most powerful. Upon arriving at Charles Town, South Carolina, he blockaded the port with his fleet. All vessels were stopped entering or leaving the port. Over the next five or six days, reports of about nine vessels were ransacked by the pirates as they attempted to sail past the Charles Town Bar where Teach's fleet was anchored.

One of those ships had a group of prominent Charles Town citizens on board including a council member named Samuel Wragg. Teach took them hostage and demanded medical supplies for his fleet. He threatened to execute all prisoners and burn all captured ships if he didn't get the supplies.

The pirates demands were presented to the Governor and the medicine was quickly gathered. Teach kept his end of the bargain and released the ships and prisoners. However, the prisoners had been relieved of their valuables and fine clothing.

While at Charles Town, Teach got word that several powerful warships had left England with orders to purge the West Indies of pirates.

<u>Queen Anne's Revenge (flagship)</u>
Teach's fleet sailed Northward along the coast and into Topsail Inlet (also known as Beaufort Inlet), North Carolina, where they intended to do repair and maintenance work on the ships. But in June of 1718, the *Queen Anne's Revenge* ran aground on a sandbar. Teach ordered the other sloops to throw ropes in an attempt to free her but at least one of those also ran aground. The damage was beyond repair. There was speculation that Teach may have ran his ship aground on purpose.

- Wreckage discovered in 1996 was thought to be Blackbeard's flagship, the *Queen Anne's Revenge*. After years of uncertainty, the North Carolina state authorities confirmed it was the ship in 2011. It sits just 25 feet underwater only a mile and a half off shore in the North Carolina waters. No pirate treasure was found however many artifacts have been recovered and are on display at the North Carolina Maritime Museum.

<u>Pardon</u>
By this time, Teach was down to two vessels and was aware of the deadline to accept the Royal

Pardon (by September 5th). However, he was unsure he would get the Pardon because of the events of Charles Town.

Keeping his plans from the crew, he confided in the Captain of the other vessel traveling with him (Bonnet). Teach felt the Governor of North Carolina (Charles Eden) was his best chance for getting the Pardon but waited to see if the other Captain would be successful in getting it first.

Bonnet left for Bath (Bath Town), North Carolina in a small sailing boat and surrendered to Governor Eden and received his Pardon. Bonnet traveled back to Beaufort Inlet to collect his boat and crew only to find Teach had striped the vessel of its valuables and provisions and had marooned the crew.

Bonnet and his crew returned to piracy and were captured before the end of that month. All but four were tried and hanged in Charles Town.

Teach had sailed on to Ocracoke Inlet, a favorite place of his to anchor. He settled in Bath where he and his much reduced crew received their Pardon from Governor Eden.

Personal Life

While in Bath (N.C.), the author Charles Johnson states that Teach married the daughter of a local plantation owner. Her name was Mary Ormond (or Ormand), she was 16 years old. It is believed that he offered her to his crew. Blackbeard may have had up to 14 common law wives however there is a lack of documentation to support this.

Death

News of Teach in area had spread and worried the Governors of the neighboring states even though it was out of their jurisdiction. They didn't think the pirates could be kept under control once they ran out of money. The Governor of Virginia, Alexander Spotswood, arranged for a party of soldiers and sailors to capture Blackbeard. There was also a reward offered.

Lieutenant Robert Maynard was given command of two sloops and told to approach the town (Bath) by sea. Maynard discovered the pirates anchored on the other side of Ocracoke Island and waited till morning to attack.

Capture of the Pirate, Blackbeard, 1718, Jean Leon Gerome Ferris, painted in 1920. (public domain)

On November 22, 1718, following a ferocious battle, Teach and some of his crew were killed by the Lieutenant and his forces.

Blackbeard's head was severed and then hung in the front of the sloop in order to collect the reward. His body was thrown into the sea.

4. Calico Jack
(1682 – 1720)

Image of Calico Jack from "A General History of the Robberies and Murders of the Most Notorious Pyrates" book published 1724. *(public domain)*

John Rackham, better known as Calico Jack, was an English pirate operating in the Caribbean, West Indies and Bahamas between 1718 - 1720. He had two female pirates in his crew named Anne Bonny (his companion) and Mary Read. His first mate, Karl Starling, had designed one of the Jolly Roger flags.

- **Calico Jack's Lost Treasure:** Though he was documented as operating in the Caribbean, there are several reports of Calico Jack burying treasure along Florida's Gulf Coast. One treasure was estimated to have 300,000 golden Mexican pesos.

- **Possible locations for his treasure are:**

    1. One such report is a ravaged ship (due to storms) that Jack and his crew found which still had "booty" on it. Some of the treasure he supposedly took and some he told the crew to bury along with the remains of the ship to retrieve at a later time. This area is currently thought to be on Marco Island (the Gulf Coast of Florida) somewhere near the Marriott.

    2. A very famous "clairvoyant" named **Edgar Cayce** (1875-1945) called the "sleeping prophet" had talked about Calico Jack's treasure while he was in a trance.

    Edgar Cayce revealed, *Rackham's booty, on the island in Lostman's River, above the tide and at the juncture of a tributary...*

much more can be read in the on-line magazine called "Venture Inward". We refer those interested to the 2016 (July/August/Sept.) issue of "Venture Inward" magazine (pages 11 – 15). Mr. Charles Thomas Cayce is on the cover of this issue of the magazine, he is Edgar Cayce's grandson.

For more information, put into your browser:
https://www.edgarcayce.org/media/6869/julsep16ventureinward.pdf

Note – The Lostman's River may be part of the Florida Everglades (state laws would apply).

Nickname and Appearance

John Rackham's nickname, Calico Jack, is believed to have come from the colorful clothing he wore. The name Jack was a common nickname for "John."

Early Life

John Rackham (alias Calico Jack) was born in Bristol, Kingdom of England in late December of 1682. Little is known about his life growing up.

Career

From about 1718, Calico Jack Rackham worked as a Quarter-Master for the infamous English pirate Captain Charles Vane (known for his cruelty) who operated in the Caribbean and the

East Coast of North America. Captain Vane's ship was called the *Ranger*.

About this time, the Governor of the Bahamas, Woodes Rogers, was authorized to grant a Royal Pardon to those pirates willing to give up their criminal ways. Captain Vane declined the Kings pardon and escaped Governor Rogers two Men of War ships by creating a diversion. He sent a fireship and fired his cannons at the ships as he slipped out of the bay.

Vane continued to capture and loot merchant vessels as he sailed along the Florida coast towards the Carolina's.

Mutiny

Tensions increased between the crew and Captain Vain concerning the plunder not being shared fairly. In November of 1718, Captain Vain was against attacking a large well armed French Man of War, as a result, the crew mutinied and promoted Calico Jack Rackham to be leader. Captain Vain and a small number of his supporters were expelled and sent off in a small sloop.

Pirate Life

Now in command, Calico Jack Rackham sailed through the Caribbean Islands where he took and plundered numerous vessels.

Off the Island of Jamaica, they took a merchant ship with a rich cargo called the *Kingston* and made it their new flagship.

They then set sail for a small island where they did maintenance on their vessel and spent their holiday (Christmas) celebrating on shore.

Off the Island of Bermuda, they were reported as taking another ship bound for England. This activity did reach Governor Rogers and after hearing of these ships being taken, he sent out a well armed and well manned sloop.

The Pirates however escaped and sailed back to Cuba, staying on shore till their provisions and money had run out.

As they prepared to leave Cuba, a Spanish Guarda del Costa appeared to have them trapped.

There are different accounts as to the events at this point, except for the pirates having lost their rich plunder in order to make their escape.

The Royal Pardon and Anne Bonny

Faced with setbacks, Calico Jack and his crew reportedly decided to accept the Royal Pardon offered by Governor Woodes Rogers. They returned to the Bahamas and their plea for the pardon was granted.

While there, he met Anne Bonny, a female pirate who was known to dress in men's clothing. At that time, Calico Jack and Anne Bonny decided to return to piracy which voided the pardon.

In August of 1720, Calico Jack commandeered a sloop named *William* from the Nassau Harbor on New Providence (Bahamas) with the help of Anne Bonny. Also joining them were other pirates. Mary Read, a female pirate who also dressed in men's clothing, was part of Calico Jack's crew however if she joined at that time is not clear.

Anne Bonny *(public domain)*

Below: Two female pirates, Anne Bonny and Mary Read by 18th century artist. (public domain)

More Pirate Life

Now cruising in the area of Jamaica, Calico Jack and his crew captured and plundered a number of small vessels.

Word reached Governor Rogers, who issued a proclamation saying that Calico Jack and his crew had returned to piracy.

Death

Soon the privateers had caught up with Calico Jack and his crew and took them into custody. They were tried and found guilty. Calico Jack was hung in Port Royal, Jamaica on November 18, 1720. His body was displayed in public (called gibbeting) as a warning to other criminals.

- According to the book, **"A General History of the Pyrates"** (Their first Rise and Settlement in the Island of Providence to the present Time) written in 1724. Anne Bonny was allowed to visit Calico Jack before his death and said to him, "she was sorry to see him there, but if he had fought like a man, he need not have been hanged like a dog."

The Female Pirates

As for Anne Bonny and Mary Read, both were convicted of Piracy on November 28th, 1720 and sentenced to death, however both were also pregnant. Their pregnancies won them a stay of execution. Read died in prison the following year but Bonny was released with no real evidence as to what happened to her at that time.

In the book **"A General History of the Pyrates"** (Their first Rise and Settlement in the Island of Providence to the present Time) written in 1724, it says about Anne Bonny; "but what is become of her since, we can not tell; only this we know, that she was not executed."

Further Research

- In November of 2020, the Youtube channel **Debunk File** may have discovered archival records for both female pirates. Found listed under **Jamaica Church of England Parish Register** are the following documents:

Burial records for "Mary Read pirate" were found on April 28, 1721 showing she died about five months after her trial.

Burial records from St. Catherine's Parish in Jamaica show a listing for an "Ann Bonny" on December, 29th, 1733.

There is a discrepancy in the spelling of Anne Bonny (Ann) but if that is the same person then she probably remained in Jamaica for 13 years after her trial. It is not known at this time what happen to her child.

5. Sir Francis Drake
(approx. 1540 - 1596)

Portrait by Marcus Gheeraerts the Younger, 1591.
(public domain)

Sir Francis Drake was an English sea captain, privateer, naval officer (Vice Admiral), slaver, pirate and a politician of the Elizabethan era. He is famous for leading the first English circumnavigation of the world from 1577 to 1580. Awarded the Knighthood in 1581 by Elizabeth I of England, he is highly respected to the English.

He was a pirate to the Spanish, who knew him as *El Draque* (Draque being Spanish for Drake) and also as *Franciscus Draco* (Latin for Francis the Dragon). He raided and plundered many Spanish ships and towns in the West Indies and along the Pacific coast of South America and more. He was humane in his treatment to prisoners.

Drake viewing treasure taken from a Spanish ship, print courtesy New York Public Library www.nypl.org (CC-BY-SA-3.0)

- **Sir Francis Drake's Lost Treasure:** In 1573, Francis Drake and his men teamed up with French privateers and successfully ambushed a 190 mule-train near Nombre de Dios (Panama). A massive amount of gold and silver was captured. They took what they could of the gold and quickly buried the excess treasure (possibly tons) before the Spanish returned.

  Drake's coffin: The British hero became sick (dysentery) and died at sea approximately 14 miles off the coast of Porto Bello, Panama in 1596. He was buried at sea dressed in his full armor and sealed inside a lead coffin. It is currently valued by the British at well over 400 million British pounds or "sterling."

- **Possible locations for his treasure are:**

  1. Nombre de Dios on the Panama isthmus and the mule trails however this town was abandoned and modern maps do not show the old town. Some maps from the 18th century may show where the "ruins" are located. A search for 16th century maps are recommended.

  2. Legends concerning treasure surround Sir Francis Drake because of the many ships and towns he plundered. One such report is a possible large treasure buried by

Drake near Arica, Chile.

3. Drakes Coffin: Two of Drake's scuttled ships have been found in the vicinity of Porto Bello, Panama but not his coffin, as of yet. See *"Further Research" at the end of this chapter.*

Early Life

Born on a Crowndale Estate/Farm in Travistock, Devon (England) in approximately 1540, Francis Drake was one of twelve children.

Edmund Drake, his father was a Protestant but due to religious persecution, the family moved to Kent (Plymouth) in 1549 where they also had family property.

The Drakes were related to the Hawkins family of Plymouth which made their living as seamen. Francis Drake began learning seamen-ship at an early age as an apprentice on the Hawkins' boats. He worked as a seamen delivering merchant goods till approximately 1566, then he joined John Hawkins on an African slave expedition.

First Command

After a successful voyage delivering slaves from West Africa to the West Indies and Spanish Main, Drake was now Captain of the *Judith* and part of a small fleet.

By this time, Spain and Portugal were aware that the British were intruding on their territory. The Spanish attacked the British fleet at San Juan de

Ulua near Mexico in 1568. Only Drakes ship and one other survived the attack and returned to England. This would be a turning point in Drakes life as he deeply resented and blamed the Spanish.

Personal Life

In 1569, Francis Drake married Mary Newman of Plymouth. She died 12 years later. In 1580, Drake purchased Buckland Abbey (a former monastery) in Devon, England where he lived while not at sea. In 1585, Drake married Elizabeth Sydenham. There were no children from either marriage.

Privateer

Though England and Spain were not at war, tensions were building. Spain did not include the English in trade with the New World. So Privateers were allowed to take what they could from Spain to benefit England.

Leaving Plymouth in May of 1572, Drake sailed in the *Swan* accompanied by a second vessel and a crew of about 70 men, bound for Panama.

On the Isthmus of Panama, known to the English as the Spanish Main, silver and gold treasure of Peru would land on one side and be sent overland by mule (Spanish silver train) to the settlement of Nombre de Dios to be picked up by Spanish Galleons (Spanish treasure fleets).

Drake arrived in Panama and explored the area on foot. He formed an alliance with the Cimaroons (also called Maroons), who were escaped African slaves. The Cimaroons showed

Drake the route the Spanish used for transporting goods and treasure.

Drake attacked the settlement of Nombre de Dios capturing its treasure and staying in the area approximately a year as he continued to raid and attack the Spanish by sea and by land. As a result, one of Drakes ships were attacked by the Spanish. Due to the attack and yellow fever, close to half the crew was dead.

In 1573, Francis Drake and his men teamed up with French privateers and successfully ambushed a 190 mule-train near Nombre de Dios. A massive amount of gold and silver in bars, coins (pesos) and other forms were captured. Unable to take it all because of the weight, they took as much gold as possible and buried as much of the excess treasure (gold /silver) as quickly as they could before the Spanish returned with more men. They traveled miles over mountains and through the jungle to get back to the coast.

Drake returned to England a very rich man but due to a temporary truce with Spain, he did not officially receive recognition for his accomplishments.

Rathlin Island Massacre

During this time, Drake was involved in the attack on Rathlin Island in Ireland. Under official orders, Sir John Norreys troops killed over 500 Scottish and Irish men, women and children while Drake's job was to prevent any reinforcements from reaching the island.

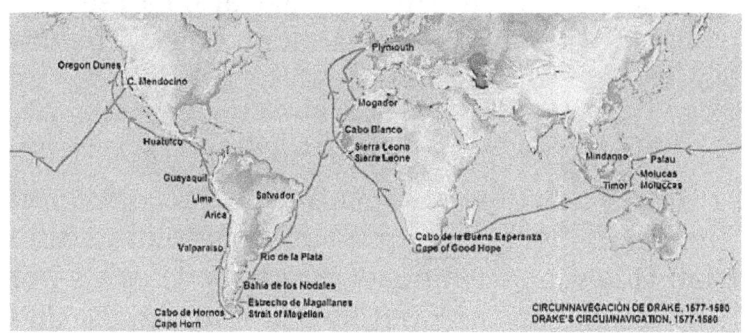

A map of Drake's route around the world. Wikimedia Commons / Continentalis / Universalis https://en.wikipedia.org/wiki/Francis_Drake#/media/File:DRAKE_1577-1580.png (CC-BY-SA-3.0)

Circumnavigation

Between 1577 – 1580, Drake set out on an expedition to explore South America and what was beyond it. He was to look for trade possibilities and to take whatever treasure he could from the Spanish.

Drake had command of five ships: *Benedict, Elizabeth, Marigold, Pelican* and *Swan*. His flagship the *Pelican,* was later renamed the *Golden Hind* during the voyage.

As the fleet sailed to the Cape Verde Islands in 1578, they captured a Portuguese Pilot named Nunho da Silva. He had knowledge in navigating the waters so he was included in the voyage. In his testimony, he recalled many ships that Drake plundered, some laden with provisions, gold and silver.

During the voyage across the Atlantic, the fleet

experienced losses from disease and storms. Two ships were scuttled (sunk). Drake also had several quarrels with a co-commander named Thomas Doughty.

The Execution of Thomas Doughty

In Port Julian, Argentina, Drake accused Thomas Doughty of mutiny and treason in a ship trial. Different accounts of this episode exists but according to one account he was found guilty and given the choice of being abandoned on a remote shore or beheaded which was the gentleman's way.

Drake tried and executed (beheaded) Thomas Doughty in 1578. Whether he had the authority for that action is a continued debate but possibly due to the Queen, Drake never stood trial for the incident.

Circumnavigation continued

Sailing down to the Strait of Magellan, the three ships passed through the Strait of Magellan in 16 days.

Now in the Pacific, bad storms caused the loss of one ship and the separation of another. The *Elizabeth* commanded by John Winter went back through the Straight of Magellan and returned to England.

Drake was now alone as he continued the voyage along the coast of Chile. Fortunately for Drake, the Spanish were completely unprepared for any threat which made it easy for Drake to seize immense treasure and plunder.

In February of 1579, Drake arrived in the harbor

of Lima (Callao, Peru), where he received news that a treasure ship had sailed just 12 days before heading for Panama. Drake immediately pursued the ship and overtook it with in a few weeks. The ship, *Nuestra Senora de la Concepcion* was to be one of Drakes largest and richest plunders yet.

From there, he continued up the coast of California where he named a northern part of California "New Albion", in reference to the white cliffs of Dover (England).

Drake stayed in the area of California for a month or so making repairs to his ship and befriending the native inhabitants.

From there, he began his voyage across the Pacific to the East Indies. Then he made his way across the Indian Ocean around the Cape of Good Hope and then finally back to Plymouth, arriving on September 26, 1580. His circumnavigation for the English a success.

Though Drake returned a hero with an enormous treasure, there was no celebration for him due to an agreement made by the Queen and King Philip of Spain. Even Drake's crew were sworn to secrecy or they risked losing their booty.

The Queens share of the treasure was more than enough to pay England's debt to foreign countries with plenty left over for the Queen and Drakes investors.

Drake was knighted by the Queen in 1581 aboard the *Golden Hind*.

The Caribbean /American Raid (1585 – 1586)
As war between Spain and England appeared imminent, Drake received orders from the Queen

to attack Spanish colonies.

With Drake in command of a large fleet (over 25 ships), they sailed from Plymouth in September of 1585. They plundered Spanish ports, taking Santiago in the Cape Verde Islands, Santo Domingo in the West Indies and St. Augustine in Florida (among others).

From St. Augustine he sailed to Roanoke Island, North Carolina where he picked up and transported a failed English settlement back to England.

The Spanish Armada

The Spanish Armada was a large fleet of ships sent by Spain in 1588 to attack and invade England.

Drake had successfully delayed the invasion by attacking the Spanish and sinking many of their ships. However, the Spanish overcame the inflicted damage and proceeded with their plans to sail up the Channel and join army transport vessels.

Drake was Vice Admiral in command of the English fleet (under Lord Howard of Effingham), as the Spanish Armada approached the shores of England.

The English fleet pursued the Armada up the Channel and a hard battle was fought.

Drake captured the galleon *Nuestra Senora del Rosario*, along with Commander Don Pedro de Valdes. The ship was reported as having carried funds to pay the Spanish Army.

Drake also carried out a daring attack on the flagship, *San Matin de Portugal*. The Armada was scattered at that point with heavy damage.

The Armada was defeated by the English and it was great victory for England.

Drakes last voyage and death

On Drakes last voyage, he was reunited with Sir John Hawkins, who had sailed with him at the beginning of his career.

Known as the Battle of San Juan (during the Anglo-Spanish War), Drake and Hawkins along with a fleet of ships tried to invade San Juan, Puerto Rico. It was a failed attempt with a fierce battle. John Hawkins had died from fever.

Drake then tried to attack Porto Bello and Panama, using Nombre de Dios on the Panama isthmus as his base. This attempt also failed.

Drake became extremely sick, but before dying he attended to his final wishes concerning his properties to his brother Thomas Drake and the others with him.

They anchored off Porto Bello, with great ships and small for the burial of Sir Francis Drake at sea. A sermon was made with all the captains of the fleet in attendance.

Further Research

More about Sir Francis Drakes coffin can be read from this news article. It's about a treasure hunting team that believe they have found two of Drakes scuttled ships and believe his coffin is somewhere in the same area.

https://www.dailymail.co.uk/news/article-2052899/Sir-Francis-Drakes-grave-verge-Panama-coast.html

6. Olivier Levasseur

(approx. 1688 – 1730)

*Concept Art of Olivier Levasseur by
Ubisoft / Marylene Pourcelot* (CC-BY-SA-4.0)
https://www.facebook.com/ArtofKatikut/photos
/a.644855595556537/644855665556530/type=3

Olivier Levasseur was a French pirate and privateer, whose aliases included Louis De Boure, Lebous, La Bouche and La Buse (The Buzzard), which referred to the quick and ruthless way he would attack his victims.

He sailed in the Indian Ocean, East Indies and more. He is known for possibly hiding one of the largest pirate treasures in history and leaving cryptic clues behind as to it's whereabouts at the time of his execution.

- **Olivier Levasseur's Lost Treasure:** According to legend, as Levasseur was about to be hanged for his crimes, he tossed a cryptogram into the crowd and said, *"My treasure for he who can understand!"*

  Reports vary as to whether it was a necklace with a cryptogram or only a piece of parchment paper with a cryptogram that was tossed into the crowd. The clue however was a 17 line cryptogram supposedly telling where his treasure was hidden. There are theories about what the cryptogram says and where the treasure might be **but it has not been recovered yet.** It is estimated to be worth over 100 million dollars and up to possibly a billion dollars.

  One of Levasseur's greatest captures was the Portuguese galleon *Nossa Senhora do Cabo* (Our Lady of the Cape) which was

◆ fully loaded with a massive treasure belonging to the Bishop of Goa and the Viceroy of Portugal, who were both on board. There were bars of gold and silver, many boxes of golden guineas, diamonds, pearls, silk, art, the Fiery Cross of Goa, religious items and more. Each pirate was said to have received over 50,000 pounds plus an estimated 42 diamonds.

Levasseur took the Fiery Cross of Goa, which was heavy pure gold inlaid with precious gems for himself and split the large remainder of booty with fellow pirate John Taylor.

◆ **Possible locations for his treasure are:**
1. The Seychelles are a group of 115 Islands in the Indian Ocean, east of Africa. The main Island of Mahe is thought to be where Levasseur's treasure is according to the Cruise-Wilkins family. They are treasure hunters who have dedicated their lives to finding Levasseur's treasure.

The father Reginald believed the code was based on masonic symbolism. Reginald Cruise-Wilkins has died but his son John continues the quest.

Others who have studied the cryptogram believe that is not the right location.

2. An island previously known as Sainte-

Marie that is now known as Nosy Boraha, off the coast of Madagascar, was the base for some of Levasseur's raids.

3. Some treasure hunters believe the treasure is likely to be on one of these six islands: Mauritius, Reunion, Fregate, Mahe, Rodrigues, Sainte-Marie.

- **Treasure Claim** - In August of 2018, two hikers found treasure on the Island of Rodrigues. This was quickly reported by the media to be the Levasseur treasure but authorities soon ruled that to be a **false claim**.

The hikers stumbled across three rocks with symbols and a gap. They returned to the same place on their next hike and took photos. They proceeded to enlarge the photos and discovered a rusty chest and a decayed rope pulley system in the gap. They did indeed find a pirates treasure however **not** Levasseur's treasure.

Treasure hunting is against the law on Rodrigues Island but because they did not excavate and it's discovery was accidental, they may be entitled to a portion of the treasure they found. The authorities had launched an investigation concerning the matter.

Alphabet of Olivier Levasseur.
Wikimedia Commons /Image by Charles.
(CC-BY-SA-3.0)

The Cryptogram of Olivier Levasseur.
(public domain)

Appearance

Levasseur's crew was said to have had a great respect for him, even though he had received an eye injury during battle that limited his vision. It also left a bad scar but did not hinder the way he lead his men.

At some point, he began wearing an eye-patch which some believe contributed to that popular pirate accessory.

He was verbally intimidating and clever, living to about 40 years of age, which was longer than many pirates.

Early Life

Levasseur was born in Calais, Northern France presumably around 1688. There is not much information about his youth but it is said that he had come from a wealthy family and was educated.

Privateer/Pirate

According to reports, Levasseur had become a naval officer for the French. During the War of Spanish Succession, he received a letter of marque from the French King, Louis XIV, to serve as a privateer. When the war had ended, he chose to continue his activities, which turned him from a privateer into a pirate.

Pirate Life

In 1716, Levasseur was captain of a sloop named *Postillion*. He and his mostly French crew headed to New Providence in the Bahamas where a group of pirates called the Flying Gang were based.

Levasseur formed an alliance with pirate captains Benjamin Hornigold and Samuel Bellamy. It was a successful venture for a while but Hornigold was an Englishman who refused to attack British ships which eventually led to the pirates going their separate ways.

Now captain of a stolen heavily gunned and larger frigate ship named the *La Louise*, Levasseur set sail for South America and Brazil attacking many ships along the way.

One attack was said to have been a slave ship coming from Angola. Levasseur took the slaves and left the crew on board to sink with the ship. After a short while, he abandoned the slaves on an island.

Fleeing from the Portuguese authorities and caught in a storm, his ship went down with about 80 men off the coast of Cotinga island in March of 1718. Levasseur survived and escaped in a smaller ship that sailed in his fleet.

Just a few months later, Levasseur reappeared in the Caribbean only to be pursued by British authorities in the *HMS Scarborough*, a 32 gun ship under the command of Captain Hume from the Royal Navy.

Escaping again with most of his fortune, Levasseur teamed up with fellow pirates Howell Davis and Thomas Cocklyn.

The three pirate captains and their fleet proceeded to attack a chief slaver port on the coast of West Africa, in the Kingdom of Whydah. They reduced the fortress to ruins. Though this raid was presumed profitable for the pirates, a much bigger prize was yet to come.

It is believed Levasseur's injured eye had become completely blind by this time because he was wearing an eye patch.

In the 1720's, Levasseur established his base on the island of Sainte-Marie, off the coast of Madagascar. He then teamed up with fellow pirates John Taylor and Jasper Seagar for one of the richest pirate captures in history.

The Portuguese galleon named *Nossa Senhora do Cabo* (translated as *Our Lady of the Cape*) was fully loaded with treasure that belonged to the Bishop of Goa and the Viceroy of Portugal, who were both on board.

The galleon had been heavily damaged in a storm so to avoid the ship from sinking, the crew had dumped all the cannons overboard. The ship then anchored off the island of Reunion for repairs.

The pirates then proceeded to board and capture the Portuguese galleon with no cannon fire.

The treasure was massive with bars of gold and silver, many boxes of golden guineas, diamonds, pearls, silk, art, the Fiery Cross of Goa, religious items and more. There was so much treasure that the pirates didn't bother to rob the passengers, something they would have normally done.

The Fiery Cross of Goa was reported as being a seven foot tall golden cross encrusted with diamonds, rubies and emeralds. It was so heavy that it took three men to carry it.

Levasseur took the Fiery Cross of Goa for himself and split the large remainder of booty with fellow pirate John Taylor. Fellow pirate Jasper Seagar died before the treasure had been divided.

Each pirate was said to have received over 50,000 pounds plus an estimated 42 diamonds.

Amnesty

In 1724, amnesty was offered to all pirates in the Indian Ocean who would give up piracy.

Levasseur sent a negotiator to the governor of the island of Bourbon (currently Reunion) to discuss amnesty but found out that the French government wanted a large part of the stolen treasure back. He rejected the terms and settled down in secret on an island in the Seychelles.

Arrested

Levasseur eventually returned to Madagascar and got work as a pilot for ships. Even though years had past since *Nossa Senhora do Cabo*, he was recognized and arrested near Fort Dauphin, Madagascar.

Death

Levasseur was taken to Saint-Denis on the island of Bourbon (currently Reunion), and was hanged for piracy at 5 pm on July 7th, 1730.

Legend says that right before Levasseur was hanged, he tossed a cryptogram into the crowd and said, *"My treasure for he who can understand!"*

Reports vary as to whether it was a necklace with a cryptogram or only a piece of parchment paper with a cryptogram that was tossed into the crowd. The clue however was a 17 line cryptogram supposedly telling where his treasure was hidden.

Further Research

If your curious about traveling to one of the islands where Levasseur may have hid his treasure, this article on the island of Reunion might provide some helpful information. The very last paragraph of this article mentions Levasseur and his treasure.

https://www.dailymail.co.uk/travel/article-3715829/An-island-R-union-m-CAROL-DRINKWATER-enchanted-natural-treasures-French-Indian-Ocean-island-vows-return-more.html

7. Amaro Rodriguez Felipe

Better known as Amaro Pargo
(1678 ? – 1747)

Anonymous portrait of Amaro Pargo from the 18th century. (public domain)

Amaro Pargo (*Spanish: a.'ma.ro 'par.yo*), was a Spanish pirate, corsair (privateer), merchant, slaver and a devout Catholic. Considered to be a sort of "Robin Hood", the booty he raised from his activities (piracy, slave trade, etc.) funded churches and charities for children, the poor, and those in prisons.

He became one of the richest men of the Canary Islands and was recognized for his service to the Spanish Crown.

- **Amaro Pargo's Lost Treasure:** Amaro had a will in which his family received a sizable fortune. Also in his will, was a description of a book marked with a "D" that itemized the contents of a carved chest with treasure. According to the will, both were in a building (or cabin) he owned (he owned numerous buildings)... the book and carved chest of treasure were **never** found.

    The carved chest was said to have contained gold jewelry, silver, pearls, gems, Chinese porcelain, fabrics and paintings.

- Amaro Pargo was said to have had many **residences** when he traveled with his fleet. He sold wine (and more) from his own vineyard to Cuba, Guyana and the Indies.
    On the way, he attacked ships belonging to the enemies of Spain and would eventually take their booty back to Spain.
    These residences and/or locations might

have treasure stashed from his raids on other ships.

◆ **Possible locations for his treasure are:**
1. Amaro Pargo's house, on the Island of Tenerife (Canary Islands) in Machado located in the municipality of El Rosario. His house has been searched by treasure hunters over the years with no treasure found.

2. The Cave of San Mateo, in the small fishing village of Punta del Hidalgo on the northeast part of Tenerife Island (Canary Islands). This cave was used by Amaro Pargo and his crew when they needed a hiding place for booty and valuables.

3. Amaro had acquired much land and many building that were rural and close to the city (San Cristobal de La Laguna), some of his properties were near a lagoon that was there at the time. The land and buildings were used for agricultural purposes and vineyards.

In 1826, the Canary Islands had a flood that prompted officials to drain the lagoon because it overflowed into the city. After that, it was said that even though the lagoon had disappeared, it would reappear during the rainy season.

That area is now a developed part of the city. An old map from approximately 1745 would be needed for investigating that possibility.

NOTE: Amaro had a large family (parents, siblings and relatives) that lived mostly on the Island of Tenerife.

Amaro was buried in a family tomb in a Roman Catholic Church (Santo Domingo de Guzman) located in the city of San Cristobal de La Laguna.
This tomb has been opened and an exhumation was carried out on the remains in 2013. After DNA testing and an investigation, the bones were returned to the tomb. **No treasure was found.**

<u>Nickname and Appearance</u>
Pargo was a nickname, which may have referred to a species of fish called the "red porgy" in English or it may have referred to his family clan.
Amaro Pargo's name, Amaro Rodríguez-Felipe y Tejera Machado is a Spanish example of a given name and two surnames. Amaro was his godfathers name, the "Rodriguez Felipe" would have referred to his father's side and the "Tejera Machado" would have referred to his mother's side.

According to DNA results from Amaro Pargo's skeleton, his height was considered "normal" at around 5 feet 4 inches and with signs of injury.

<u>Early Life</u>
Amaro Pargo was born in San Cristobal de La Laguna, on the Island of Tenerife (Canary

Islands). He was the son of Juan Rodriguez Felipe and Beatriz Tejera Machado, and was baptized at the *Iglesia de Los Remedios* (Church of Los Remedios).

We include a question mark with his birth date (1678 ?). The reason for this is (in general) the favored date for his birth date seems to be 1678, however, a different date can also be found in research.

Amaro's family was large and included many brothers, sisters and relatives that lived close to each other and the city. His sisters entered the Convent of Santa Catalina de Siena.

As a young man (teen), Amaro exhibited responsibility and good judgment to his father both on land and by sea. He made trips to Cuba and Venezuela to export wine and other products.

First Command

In 1701, he was reported as having served on a ship called the Ave Marie, nicknamed La Chata (the Barge). This was a galley ship of the King of Spain on route between Spain and the Caribbean.

Being boarded by pirates, Amaro advised the Captain to fake a surrender in order to launch a surprise attack. This strategy worked in which they emerged victorious.

Out of gratitude, the Captain gave Amaro his first ship. He used this ship to expand his many business activities including participating in the African slave trade. In addition, he also received a letter of marque from King Philip V of Spain (Spanish: Felipe).

A few years later, he was documented as being captain and owner of a frigate and participating in the West Indies fleet.

Privateer/Pirate

Now part of the West Indies fleet, Amaro used the opportunity to export his own harvest of wine, brandy and more, which he sold in Havana and Guyana.

On these voyages, he would attack ships that were enemies of Spain. This included the British and the Dutch. He also fought against well known pirates including Blackbeard. He was successful in confiscating the booty from these enemy ships which he eventually brought back to Spain.

Amaro Pargo was appointed Captain of several large vessels, at times by Royal orders.

Nobility

Amaro applied for recognition of the nobility of his family and obtained it.

In 1727, Amaro received the certification of nobility and arms under King Philip V of Spain.

Personal Life

Amaro had become romantically involved with two woman but did not marry either. Each woman had a child.

Amaro lived with a Cuban woman named Josefa Ma del Valdespino, when he went to Havana, Cuba. The woman was wealthy with several houses, slaves and more. There was no talk of marriage, she was considered to be a "lover" (and reported as already married). She had a son named Manuel de la Trinidad in which Amaro Pargo was the father. However, Amaro's family did not accept him as being family.

The second woman was also married, but had known Amaro and his family for a long time. She had a son named Juan Rodriguez Felipe and he was raised by Amaro's mother. That child was accepted by Amaro's family.

Mary of Jesus de León y Delgada

Sister Mary of Jesus, the spiritual counselor of Amaro Pargo (public domain)

Amaro had a close friendship with a nun known as Mary of Jesus de León y Delgada. He claimed the nun had miraculously intervened on many of his exploits by way of a phenomenon called bilocation (in two places at the same time).

Though she never left the convent, he credited her with saving his life while in Cuba. Amaro was so grateful to her that he paid for an extravagant sarcophagus at the time of her death in which he carved his initials in the sarcophagus.

- <u>Mary of Jesus de León y Delgada:</u> had a simple but remarkable life with many miracles that were attributed to her such as levitation, ecstasy, bilocation, clairvoyance, healing and more.

<u>Death and Inheritance</u>

In 1747, Amaro died in his hometown. His funeral had a crowd that accompanied his body to his burial site. He was buried at the Santo Domingo de Guzman Convent in his family tomb in La Luguna.

Engraved on his headstone was his family's shield, under that was a skull with a winking right eye and crossbones.

Amaro's estate was worth a substantial amount when he died. His Cuban son appeared and wanted his part of the inheritance but his claims were rejected by the rest of Amaro's heirs.

8. Spanish Treasure Fleet (1715)

*"Spanish Galleon" Artwork courtesy
of Cactus Cowboy via openclipart (.org)
https://openclipart.org/artist/cactus%20cowboy*

In July of 1715, the Spanish Treasure Fleet (also known as the Spanish Plate Fleet or Spanish Silver Fleet) was going to Spain from Havana, Cuba, loaded with an enormous fortune for the King of Spain, Philip V. A powerful hurricane came across the Bahama channel and hit the fleet.

Of the 12 ships, only one ship survived, a French vessel named *"Le Grifon"* whose Captain was not familiar with the Florida coast and chose to go to deeper waters. The rest of the ships (Spanish) either capsized or broke into pieces on the coral reefs along the east coast of Florida during the hurricane. Records differ but are estimated at well over a thousand lives lost.

This area of Florida, where the 1715 fleet went down, is known as **"The Treasure Coast"**. It includes Fort Pierce, Sebastian Inlet and Vero beach.

- **The Spanish Treasure Fleets lost treasure:** The Spanish treasure fleet were two separate fleets that sailed together, there was also one French ship on this voyage.

    Though both fleets carried treasure, General Ubilla's fleet (5 ships) was believed to be carrying the **most** treasure.

    Registered items included large numbers of chests filled with silver coins, gold coins, gold bars, gold dust, precious gems, pearls, jewelry, and exquisite porcelain. Additional cargoes had also been loaded.

Also included in this treasure was a dowry for the King of Spain's new wife (in her early 20's), which was a magnificent treasure all by itself. It included many pieces of rare jewelry made of precious gems and pearls.

The Spanish also had a very hefty tax on all registered items which was a very good reason to smuggle as much as possible.

This was a large fleet exceptionally loaded with treasure for the King of Spain... we believe there is **much more treasure** waiting to be discovered.

- Here is some more information, during the late 1600's, Europe had been at war for over 20 years.
  Due to the "The War of the Spanish Succession" (1701 - 1714), the King of Spain Philip V, was in critical need of this treasure shipment arriving safely, his resources had been depleted.
  Though an agreement for peace (known as the Peace of Utrecht) had been reached, the sea was still a dangerous place for Spanish ships carrying treasure.

- **Possible locations for the treasure are:** The area along the coast line of

Florida (U.S.) known as "The Treasure Coast" that are **in the water,** are under jurisdiction. Check with authorities in that County (or area) first, if your interest involves scuba diving.

However, along the beaches of "The Treasure Coast" of Florida, discoveries from the 1715 fleet are still happening today by beach-goers.

One of the best ways to search for this kind of treasure is to keep an eye on the weather and ocean conditions. After a storm and/or rough waves that stir up the ocean floor, is when treasure is sometimes washed ashore onto the shoreline or beach.

Note: We made a trip ourselves in the beginning of 2021 to try some treasure hunting in this area. We went to the "Turtle Trail Beach Access" where reports of silver coins from 1715 had been found.
Though we were not successful ourselves that day with finding fleet coins, we did enjoy the trip! By the way, that place has multiple surveillance cameras around so be careful about following the rules (such as keeping off the dunes).

<u>Recovery Efforts by Spain</u>

After the hurricane hit, a few survivors had walked along the beach to get to St Augustine, there they learned the fate of the other vessels.
The Spanish authorities had heard the news and

quickly responded with salvage crews, more for the treasure than for any survivors.

- During the Spanish recovery efforts, many ships and pirates participated.

Henry Jennings, an English privateer that had turned to piracy (along with his crew) was accused of piracy during the Spanish recovery efforts of the 1715 fleet. He sailed with other well known pirates such as "Black Sam" Bellamy.

A large amount of treasure (pieces of eight, etc.) had been recovered by the Spanish. Their recovery efforts had taken a few years to complete. They claimed they had retrieved the registered items. The problem with their claim was their efforts did not include all the ships that went down or the smuggled items.

Current Recovery Efforts

As of this writing, seven of the Spanish ships are believed to have been found, two ships are still lost at sea and two other ships have been found with new evidence about one of those ships.
The French vessel *"Le Grifon"* had returned safely to France after the hurricane.

The Fleet

The Spanish fleet consisted of two separate fleets.

The Nueva Espana fleet (New Spain fleet) was under the command of General Don Juan Esteban de Ubilla.

The Terra Firme fleet was under the command of General Don Antonio de Echeverz y Zubiza.

General Ubilla's Nueva Espana Fleet

1. *Nuestra Señora de la Regla* – (Our Lady of Rule) known as the Cabin Wreck.

2. *Santo Cristo de San Roman* - (Holy Christ of Saint Roman) known as the Corrigan's Wreck.

3. *Urca De Lima* (Santissima Trinidad) – *Urca de Lima* (Holy Trinity) known as the Wedge Wreck.

4. * *Nuestra Senora de las Nieves* – (Our Lady of the Snows) known as the Colored Beach Wreck.

5. * *Nuestra Señora de la Regla* - Ubilla's personal Cuban boat he renamed the same name as his flagship.

New Evidence

* The Colored Beach Wreck (Gold Wreck or Douglas Wreck) was thought to be the *"Nuestra Senora de las Nieves"* (ship 4.) but now may also include General Ubilla's personal boat *"Nuestra Señora de la Regla"* (ship 5.).

General Echeverz Terra Firme fleet

1. *Nuestra Senora del Carmen* – (Our Lady of Carmen) known as the Rio Mar Wreck.

2. *Nuestra Senora del Rosario* – (Our Lady of the Rosary) known as the Sandy Point Wreck.

3. ** *San Miguel / Nuestra Senora de La Popa* – (Our Lady of La Popa) a captured Dutch sloop formally known as *La Holandsea*. This site is known as the La Holandesa Wreck.

4. *Sr. San Miguel* also known as *El Senor San Miguel*.

5. *Nuestra Senora de la Concepcion* (Our Lady of the Conception).

6. ** *La Galleria* – a captured French frigate formally known as *El Ciervo*.

** General Echeverz captured these two ships and added them to the fleet. He renamed them *San Miguel* (ship 3.) and *La Galleria* (ship 6.).

Areas of Interest

The general area of the ship wrecks are near Vero beach, Florida (US). Beginning at Melbourne beach or Sebastian Inlet, going south at least 5 miles past Fort Pierce Inlet should be considered areas of interest for beach metal detecting and treasure hunting.

Colored Beach Wreck (Gold Wreck or Douglas Wreck) is believed to be approximately 1 to 3 miles south of Fort Pierce Inlet.

The missing ships *Sr, San Miguel* and *La Galleria* are thought to have possibly gone down near the Georgia / Florida border.

Another Ship Lost

The *Maria Galante* – was a small one mast ship that may have been part of the 1715 Treasure Fleet. Also lost in the hurricane, it is known as the Cannon Wreck. It is presumed to be near Treasure Shores Beach Park on Vero beach.

Cannon Dedication

In February of 2022, a cannon that had been recovered from the 1715 Spanish treasure fleet was unveiled at the Melody Lane Fishing Pier Plaza in Fort Pierce, Florida.

With a crowd attending and media coverage, the Mayor and others spoke at the event that unveiled a beautiful cannon and a large informative display for the public to enjoy

9. Jean Lafitte - Wild Card
(approx. 1782 – ?)

Anonymous portrait of Jean Lafitte, early 19th century, Rosenberg Library, Galveston, Texas
(public domain)

Due to information on Lafitte's death that contradicts historical records, he is our **"Wild Card"** pick... however we do still believe he has **lost treasure** just waiting to be found!

Jean Lafitte was a French pirate, privateer, spy, naval officer, diplomat and businessman that sailed in the Gulf of Mexico during the early 1800's.

- **Jean Lafitte's Lost Treasure:** Tales of buried treasure from Lafitte are rumored in many locations, including Texas, along coastal Louisiana and in Florida.
Jean Lafitte operated a warehouse for smuggled goods in New Orleans, then later moved that to the Grand Terre Island in Barataria Bay, Louisiana. He and his brother Pierre had an expanding business which included piracy and the slave trade among other things. Jean Lafitte also had a colony and smuggling base in Texas.
Favored by local merchants that benefited from their operation, the Lafitte's found clever ways of running their business. **Millions of dollars were earned annually from stolen and smuggled goods and treasures.** So much in fact, that the government felt as though they were getting only a small amount of what was actually owed.

Jean Lafitte and his men defended New Orleans in the Battle of New Orleans (1812) against the British in exchange for a full pardon for him and his men, this was granted by President James Madison.

Jean Lafitte's possible faked death:

According their book, *Jean Laffite Revealed,* authors Ashley Oliphant and Beth Yarbrough spent approximately two years gathering information about the faked death of Jean Lafitte.

They say he faked his death in the Caribbean in the 1820's, then went to Cuba for a while. He eventually reappeared in Mississippi under the false name of Lorenzo Ferrer (or Lorendzo Ferrier). From there, he moved to Lincolnton, North Carolina where he lived from 1839 - 1875. This would have meant he lived to approximately 95 - 96 years old.

- More information about the book *Jean Laffite Revealed* can be found on YouTube: https://www.youtube.com/watch?v=vKUOqceHj68

Old newspaper articles for that area of North Carolina can be accessed on-line that reveal the local residents thought he was either Lafitte himself or one of his commanders. It also mentions he did not work, he kept to himself and he did have treasure.

There is one account of him asking a close friend to help him move one or more treasure chests to safer grounds because of a conflict in that area.

Is this important and does it concern his **"lost treasure"... absolutely!**

If Jean Lafitte had faked his death, going back to any place he had treasure stashed would have jeopardized everything. His enemies and victims would have recognized him, it was a very high risk.

- **Possible locations for his treasure are:**
  1. The Mermentau River and Calcasieu River in Louisiana were used by Lafitte, according to a slave from that time, several caches were buried in those areas.

  2. The Sabine River, which runs along the states of Texas and Louisiana and then into Lake Sabine, was said to have been one of the pirate's favorite retreats.
  There is a tale of a large cache said to be somewhere on the Sabine River close to a grove of gum trees, roughly 3 miles east of the Old Spanish Trail.

  3. Grand Terre Island in Barataria Bay, Louisiana, where Jean Lafitte had his smuggling operation, has had reports of coins found from that era. This Island is accessible only by boat.

4. The Island of Campeche (now Galveston) in Texas is where Jean Lafitte, his brother and their pirate associates spent approximately three years. They raided a great number of merchant ships in the Gulf of Mexico during that time. Lafitte's headquarters on the Island was a building painted red and surrounded by a moat called *Maison Rouge*.

Due to charges against one of his pirate captains, Lafitte was pressured by the government to leave the island. Jean Lafitte agreed to leave but set fire to the settlement upon departure. According to legend, they were said to have stashed caches of loot in various places before they actually set sail from the area.

5. Fowler's Bluff in Florida is still believed to have lost treasure that many believe is Lafitte's. Tales of treasure continue to linger and treasure hunts funded by investors have continued on and off for years in that area. See **_Treasure Claim #3_**.

6. Lake Borgne in Louisiana was a lake according to older maps, however the terrain has changed over time due to coastal erosion. There is a tale of a large lost cache that may be located on an island that is unnamed somewhere in the area of Lake Borgne.

♦ **Treasure Claim #1** – In 1923, a work-crew foreman, while digging a culvert, found three metal boxes of French, English and Spanish coins made of both silver and gold and minted in the 1700's. These were found on Jefferson Island (formerly known as Orange Island in the 1800's) in Louisiana. The foreman attempted to steal the treasure however the owner of the property found out about the discovery. The owner tracked down the foreman and was able to recover some of the treasure which is now on display on the island.

A knife traditionally used by pirates from the 17th and 18th centuries was also found on the property. The knife and the treasure are believed to likely be from Lafitte.

Treasure Claim #2 - In 1921, and in the same area of Jefferson Island, a newspaper article for New Orleans said supposed treasure had been found and the evidence for this were several gold coins that had found their way into circulation bearing the date 1754. The article also said there was much commotion about it and the treasure finders were being silent on the discovery.

Treasure Claim #3 – Florida: According to an article from 1945 in The Evening Post, pirates would stop by Fowler's Bluff (near the southern end of the Suwanee River) in Florida to careen their ships and hang out in the early 1800's. Jean Lafitte,

Jose Gaspar and Black Caesar were said to have stopped there.

In 1888, a man named Emmett Baird arrived in Fowler's Bluff with a treasure map he'd received from an old man on his deathbed.

While in the process of recovering the treasure, he disappeared from Fowler's Bluff and showed up in Gainesville, Florida with enough money to start a bank and open a hardware store bearing his name.

Many believe the rumor that he struck it rich at Fowler's Bluff. Though there is no proof, many also believe it may have been Jean Lafitte's treasure.

It is said about Lafitte that when he went to bury treasure, he would take one person with him, once the treasure was buried he would kill that person so his ghost would guard the treasure. It is not known if this is based on truth or speculation.

Appearance and Name

Jean Lafitte was clever and resourceful with a natural ability for leadership. He cared about the way he dressed and enjoyed drinking, gambling and women.

Jean Lafitte and his brother Pierre spelled their last name **Laffite**, however English documents spelled it as **"Lafitte"** which became the common spelling in the United States.

Early Life
Details are not clear about Jean Lafitte's early life or where he was born. A popular claim is he was born in the French colony of Saint-Domingue (now Haiti) and migrated to New Orleans with his widowed mother and his older brother Pierre during the 1780's.

According to his "journal" (which some contest it's authenticity), he was born in Bordeaux, France.

Still, there are other claims speculating different locations for his birthplace. Being a native of France (at that time) provided a convenient protection from certain laws.

Education
It is believed that Jean Lafitte and his brother had a military education from an academy on an island in the west indies known as Saint Kitts. Their knowledge of artillery would later be commended by Andrew Jackson in the Battle of New Orleans (War of 1812) against the British.

He spoke French, English and probably Spanish.

The Embargo Act of 1807
The Lafitte's operation was the distribution of smuggled goods from a warehouse in New Orleans. When the Embargo Act of 1807 passed, they moved their operation to an island in Barataria Bay, Louisiana.

Barataria
Barataria island, located between several barrier islands in Louisiana, made it easy to continue

smuggling without being noticed. Those that worked there called themselves the Baratarians. By 1810, they had achieved much success and a thriving port.

Privateer/Pirate

On June 18, 1812, the United States declared war on Britain (War of 1812). The British Royal Navy was powerful, so the United States offered letters of marque to privately armed vessels, authorizing them to capture ships and submit their booty to the American authorities to supplement revenue.

In New Orleans, the letters of marque were mainly answered by smugglers who worked with Lafitte at Barataria. They would submit booty from captured British ships but not booty from other ships, that booty would often be smuggled through Lafitte's operation. This was noticed by American authorities.

Arrested

In November of 1812, the government sent soldiers to Barataria. Jean Lafitte, his brother Pierre and more than 20 smugglers were arrested and charged with "violation of revenue law." Officials released the smugglers after they posted bail only to have them disappear and refuse to return for trial.

Charges were brought against Pierre and a Grand Jury indicted him after testimony from a city merchant. Pierre was jailed while Jean Lafitte continued to run the business.

British

By this time, the British had established a base in Pensacola, Florida and increased their patrols in the Gulf of Mexico. One of the British Navy ships fired upon Lafitte's ship (associate), returning to Barataria. The larger British ship could not go into the shallow waters and raised a white flag. They then launched a dinghy with several officers in hopes of a meeting. Lafitte and several of his men rowed out to meet them halfway.

The Captain of the British ship, accompanied by an infantry Captain, had been ordered to contact the "Commandant at Barataria" and deliver a message. The Baratarians invited them to their island, once they disembarked, Lafitte identified himself. The smugglers wanted to lynch the British but Lafitte intervened and ensured their protection.

Two letters for Lafitte were brought, one from King George III that offered British citizenship and land grants, the other was from a Lieutenant Colonel urging him to accept.

At this time, Lafitte was also aware that the Americans feared he might side with the British and that the Americans were planing to attack Barataria.

Lafitte believed the U.S. would eventually win against Great Britain. He told the British he would need 15 days to review their offer, during which time he had copies of the letters and a personal note sent out to a member of the state legislature who had invested in his operation.

He also gently reminded him that his brother was still in jail.

Lafitte pledged his help and the help of his men for the defense of New Orleans... Pierre "escaped" from jail shortly afterwards.

Attack on Barataria

As expected, the U.S. ordered an attack on Barataria in September of 1814. The USS Carolina was accompanied by approximately six gunboats.

The pirates formed a battle line but it wasn't long before the pirates abandoned their ships, set fire to a few ships and fled. Jean Lafitte had successfully escaped. The Americans proceeded to take custody of numerous ships, cannons and goods worth at least $500,000.

Louisianans

The Governor of Louisiana wrote the U.S. Attorney General and requested a pardon for the Baratarians, stating that the people of Louisiana felt they had "helped them for generations" and they had sympathy for them. He also stated that Lafitte had offered to defend Louisiana (New Orleans) against the British, something that was now potentially destroyed.

Battle of New Orleans

In December of 1814, Andrew Jackson arrived in New Orleans and discovered that New Orleans was not prepared for a British attack. Even though the city had confiscated ships (formerly Lafitte's), there weren't enough sailors to man them.

Lafitte's men resented the attack on Barataria and refused to serve on their former ships.

Andrew Jackson met with Lafitte, who offered to defend the city in exchange for a full pardon for him and his men. Jackson agreed to the terms and with Lafitte's encouragement, many of his men joined and served.

The Treaty of Ghent, which formally ended the War of 1812, was signed on December 24th, 1814. However the news had not yet reached the United States for several weeks.

Andrew Jackson commended the Barataria men and their Captains Renato Beluche and Dominique Youx (Youx was believed to be related to Lafitte), for their great skill with artillery. Jackson also said Jean and Pierre Lafitte "exhibited the same courage and fidelity." They were granted a full pardon by President James Madison.

Galveston

In late 1815 - 1816, the Lafitte brothers agreed to act as spies for Spain. Pierre was to inform about New Orleans and Jean was sent to Galveston island.

After a few weeks at Galveston, Jean returned to New Orleans to report his activities. With Spanish permission, he returned to Galveston promising to continue the reports.

At that time, Galveston was part of Spanish Texas and part of Mexico. The U.S. did not have authority there.

Lafitte took command of the island and appointed his own officers. He flew the flag of Mexico but did not want to be part of the revolution. He developed the island into another smuggling base and called it *Campeche*.

As the colony grew, it had more than two thousand inhabitants and an annual income of over $2 million (equivalent to over $35 million today) in stolen goods and currency.

The colony suffered due to a hurricane in 1818 which resulted in flooding, damage and death.

After approximately three years, Lafitte was pressured to leave Campeche by the government because of charges against one of his pirate captains. He agreed to leave but had his men set the buildings on fire first.

Personal Life

It is believed that Jean Lafitte did have at least one child (probably more).

A popular account of Jean Lafitte was that he was involved with the sister of his brothers mistress. She was a free woman of color who gave birth to a son, on November 4th 1815. Later accounts show a possible death of the boy in New Orleans, due to a cholera epidemic at the time.

Another popular account, according to his "Journal" (which some contest it's authenticity), is Lafitte got married young and had three children. The mother died in childbirth after the last child.

Later in life, Lafitte married again and had two more sons that possibly took on an assumed name.

After Campeche

Many of Lafitte's men thought he had a valid commission to privateer, however after the arrest of several of his men, the truth was revealed.

Though about half his crew left, he continued to attack the Spanish ships and often returned to the areas near New Orleans to unload the cargo.

In 1822, Lafitte approached Great Columbia, who was hiring former privateers to be officers in their navy. Lafitte was accepted and was now legally authorized to take Spanish ships. He was also given a 43-ton schooner to command.

Speculated Death

In 1823, Lafitte was sailing in his schooner near Omoa, Honduras. Omoa had a large Spanish fort built to guard Spanish silver shipments.

Lafitte attempted to take two Spanish merchant vessels during the evening hours in that area however they turned back and attacked him.

Lafitte was believed to have died just after dawn and was buried at sea.

10. José Gaspar – Real or Myth
(approx. 1756 – 1821)

José Gaspar as illustrated in the 1900 brochure: advertising brochure for railroad line and Boca Grande Resort - (public domain)

José Gaspar – Real or Myth:

Although some give credit to José Gaspar for certain "lost" treasures... after close examination, we think this pirate may be more "mythical" than real.

So much concerning José Gaspar are tales that can not be confirmed. In fact, there seems to be only one main source, a man named Juan Gomez (also known as John Gomez).

Mr. Gomez was a fishing guide in Pinellas County, Florida during the time that "The Story of Gasparilla" was first published.

These sort of tales were said to be something he used to entertain his customers on trips. How much actual "truth" were in these stories is not known.

Needless to say, Mr. Gomez must have been very convincing because those who heard his "tales" retold them to others.

A company called the Charlotte Harbor and Northern Railway printed "The Story of Gasparilla" as a marketing item for the Gasparilla Inn in the resort town of Boca Grande. It featured the pirate José Gaspar. This worked well for the Hotel since it was located on Gasparilla Island.

Gasparilla Island was named after a Friar (Spanish churchman). The island's name appears on older maps before the time of the pirate José Gaspar.

From there, the mystery of José Gaspar continued to grow and soon became folklore for Florida's West Coast.

11. Gasparilla Pirate Festival

(1904 – current)

The pirate ship José Gasparilla (Gasparilla II) sailing into downtown Tampa to start the Gasparilla parade. (image by Christopher Hollis) (public domain)

Hosted by the City of Tampa, Florida (U.S.)

- The main event or "pirate invasion" by José Gaspar and his crew, takes place on the last Saturday in January (check schedule).
- "Gasparilla Season" runs approximately from January to March.

12. Popular Pirate Festivals

There are **many** notable Pirate Festivals in the U.S. and around the world!

Arrr matey... here we list just a **few** popular Pirate Festivals that pirate enthusiasts might like to know about, if they didn't know already!

Due to current events (such as the pandemic), some great festivals were discontinued but these festivals are still active (at the time of this writing). Always check scheduled events for current times and dates before going.

Florida Pirate Festivals (U.S.)

- **Gasparilla Pirate Festival** – in Tampa, Fl. (since 1904) The main event or "pirate invasion" features a large pirate ship with it's flotilla! Generally on the last Saturday in January. "Gasparilla Season" features other events from January – March.
- **Billy Bowlegs Festival** – in Fort Walton Beach, Fl. An annual event for over 60 years! This is a hearty celebration that features a pirate invasion and downtown party, a torchlight parade, craft beers by local brewers and a children's pirate play zone! On the first weekend in May or June.

- **Pirates of the High Seas Festival** - Panama City Beach, Fl. Featuring storytelling, exciting staged pirate battles, treasure hunts, fireworks, pirate activities and more. This annual pirate event happens in October.

More Pirate Festivals (U.S.)

- **Contraband Days Louisiana Pirate Festival** - Based on the legend of Jean Lafitte, this is for two weeks with more than a 100 events! Held in Lake Charles, Louisiana from April 28th to May 10th.
- **Blackbeard Pirate Festival** – Recently named the 3rd best pirate festival in North America by USA Today. Blackbeard and his pirates are part of a loaded schedule of festivities. Normally on June 4th - 5th in Hampton, Virginia.
- **Tybee Island Pirate Fest** – This festival features live music, pirate performers, a parade, vendors, great food and fun for all ages! This 3 day event is held usually in the beginning of October on Tybee Island in Georgia.
- **Pirates Of The Pacific Festival** – This festival began in 2011 and features live music, pirates, mermaids and a full events schedule. Held for 3 days in mid-August on the Boardwalk, Port of Brookings Harbor in Oregon.

Worldwide Pirate Festivals

- **Pirate Week in the Cayman Islands** – A popular 11 day pirate event with pirates landing in George Town harbor, parades, street dancing, games, food, music and much more! Held in mid-November (book rooms well in advance).
- **Brixham Pirate Festival in South Devon (U.K.)** - This festival began in 2007 and has grown to be one of Britain's biggest pirate celebrations. Authentic Pirate and Naval seaside festivities that includes lots of scheduled entertainment and pirate-themed family fun. The 3-day event is normally on April 30th – May 2nd.

Miscellaneous

- **Talk Like A Pirate Day** – An International Day that celebrates pirates and their language! On September 19th.

13. Treasure Hunting Quick Tips

- Do your research! The more you can find out by doing research first... the better!

- Take what you need but try to travel light.

- Water is an essential item. Check your drinks and food before your trip.

- Check batteries if your equipment uses that, also bring extra batteries if needed.

- Use the buddy system if possible and find someone to go on your trip with you.

- Let someone know where you are going and when you'll return.

- Check any medications you may need and be sure to bring them if they are needed.

- Consider the area that your going to and what dangers or obstacles might be there. For example, could there be poison ivy, mosquitoes, or maybe snakes. To prepare, wear an appropriate pair of shoes, bring bug spray or bring a pair of latex gloves.

TEMPLATE

14. Treasure Hunting Log Book

Entry #1:

Date:

Location:

Finds:

Notes:

Entry #2:

Date:

Location:

Finds:

Notes:

Glossary

Amnesty is a decision by a government or an authority to forgive and not punish people who have committed illegal acts or crimes. An amnesty constitutes more than a pardon, in so much as it obliterates all legal remembrance of the offense.

Buccaneer is basically an unsanctioned privateer or free sailor that may have committed acts of piracy which often times were allowed by the government.

Careening (also known as "heaving down") is the practice of using the receding tide (or shallow water) to ground a vessel, in order to expose one side of its hull for maintenance, repairs and cleaning below the waterline. At high tide, the ship resumes it's up-right normal position.

Cat o' nine tails was a short type of whip used that featured nine knotted strands of rope that connected to the main handle.

Code of Conduct (pertaining to pirates) – was a set of rules pirates were expected to follow on a vessel or as part of a crew.

Cutlass – is a short curving sword.

Fire-ship – is a ship that has been set on fire and is sometimes used as a diversion.

Flogging or "whipping" usually on the back, was punishment at sea commonly used for enforcing rules and subduing prisoners both on pirate ships and on military ships of many nations.

Flotilla – is a group or fleet of ships or boats.

Frigate – were generally used as naval warships, they had a long hull design for speed. In the 17th and 18th century, they were fast three mast sailing ships (some with oars) armed with approximately 30 or more guns.

Galleon – is a large sailing ship having three or more masts with a square rig and several decks. Used from the 15th to the early 18th century as warships or merchant ships, especially by the Spanish.

Gaol – means jail. The historical origin of this word is thought to be British or European, it is not commonly used nowadays.

Gibbet (or Gibbet cage, Gibbeted hanging) – is a chain or metal-slat cage in which pirate corpses are hung and displayed in order to discourage piracy.

Impressment – (also known as pressing) is the taking of men for service, usually into a military or naval force by compulsion, with or without notice.

Isthmus of Panama is a narrow strip of land that lies between the Caribbean and the Pacific Ocean linking North and South America.

Man-Of-War – (also Man-O-War) is a warship heavily armed for battle and usually propelled by sails. Often historically associated with the British Navy.

Marooned – is to be stranded or left behind, usually on a desert island or a remote location.

Pardon – is to be released from the penalty of an offense or to forgive an error.

Per stirpes – are equal shares to each member of a specified class with the share of a deceased member divided proportionately among his or her beneficiaries (such as children).

Pinnace – is a small boat with sails or oars used to go to shore or to another ship. Often used as a service boat for a larger vessel.

Piracy is an act of robbery at sea on a ship or a coastal area, typically to attack and steal cargo and valuable goods.

Pirate – is someone who attacks and steals or commits acts of piracy.

Plate – (Spanish meaning) is derived from the Spanish word "plata" for silver.

Privateer is a private person or ship under a government commission that gives them the legal authority to commit acts of piracy. Sometimes pirates were employed by governments for these positions.

Schooner – is a fore-and-aft rigged sailing vessel with two or more masts, the larger mast toward the center and the smaller mast toward the front.

Scuttle – (scuttled, scuttling) means to sink a ship on purpose (deliberately). Reasons may include to prevent a ship from being captured by the enemy or to dispose of the ship.

Sloop – is a fore-and-aft rigged sailing vessel with one mast and a small triangle head-sail (called jib). Favored by pirates because they were fast and easy to maneuver.

Spanish Main – are lands taken and claimed by Spain (the Spanish Empire) from Mexico to Peru including some Caribbean islands (also known as the Spanish West Indies).

Spanish Treasure fleet – (also known as the West Indies fleet or silver fleet) were Spanish convoys of general purpose cargo fleets used for transporting a wide variety of items such as gold, silver, gems, pearls, spices, sugar, tobacco, silk, agricultural goods and more. Spanish goods such as oil, wine and more were transported in the opposite direction.

A system of sea routes by the Spanish Empire were used to connect Spain with it's territories in the Americas and as a transatlantic trade route.

Weigh anchor is a nautical term indicating the final preparation of a sea vessel for getting underway.

Weighing anchor literally means raising the anchor of the vessel from the sea floor and hoisting it up to be stowed on board the vessel. At the moment when the anchor is no longer touching the sea floor, it is aweigh.

West Indies fleet – *See Spanish Treasure Fleet.*

Research and Resources

We would like to thank all those who helped to make this book possible (we are eternally grateful), thank you so much.

Primary sources, such as original documents, records, manuscripts, archives, articles, etc. were used in an effort to provide as much factual information as possible.

Secondary sources, in addition to our own knowledge gathered through the years, were also checked for accuracy when possible.

General Resources

- Library of Congress: https://www.loc.gov/
- British History Online: https://www.british-history.ac.uk
- Patagonia Bookshelf: http://patlibros.org
- Google: https://www.google.com/
- Google Translate: https://translate.google.com/
- The Internet Archive: https://archive.org/
- Youtube: https://www.youtube.com/
- Wikipedia: https://en.wikipedia.org/

eBooks

- Gosse, Philip (1924) The pirates' who's who - London, England (Dulau & Co.)

- Johnson, Capt. Charles [pseud.] (1724) A General History of the Robberies and Murders of the Most Notorious Pyrates: 2nd ed. London (T. Warner)

Societies
- The Drake's Exploration Society: http://www.indrakeswake.co.uk/Society/index.htm
- 1715 Fleet Society: https://1715fleetsociety.com
- The Lafitte Society: http://thelaffitesociety.com/index.html

Libraries
- East Hampton Library/Long Island Collection (Receipt for Treasure found on Gardiner's Island – *Capt. Kidd*): http://easthamptonlibrary.org/long-island-history/digital-long-island/
- Jean Laffitte, The Journal of Jean Laffite, a manuscript currently housed at Sam Houston Regional Library and Research Center, Liberty, Texas.

Further Research:
- Article: Did Sussex Bounty Hunter Dig up Captain Kidd's Treasure? from Daily Mail https://www.dailymail.co.uk/news/article-2235400/Did-Sussex-bounty-hunter-dig-Captain-Kidds-treasure-Hunt-12m-haul-gold-coins

- Article: Henry Every alias John Avery in "The Saba Islander" by Will Johnson from https://thesabaislander.com/2018/10/04/henry-every-alias-john-avery
- Article: Search For Pirate's Treasure on Lostman's River in "Venture Inward" mag. https://www.edgarcayce.org/media/6869/julsep16ventureinward.pdf
- Debunk File Channel (Youtube) on Mystery solved as to what happened to Calico Jack's female pirate companion Anne Bonny.
- Article: Drakes Coffin from Daily Mail https://www.dailymail.co.uk/news/article-2052899/Sir-Francis-Drakes-grave-verge-Panama-coast.html
- Article: https://www.dailymail.co.uk/travel/article-3715829/An-island-R-union-m-CAROL-DRINKWATER-enchanted-natural-treasures-French-Indian-Ocean-island-vows-return-more.html
- North Carolina's digital collection of news articles and more https://digital.ncdcr.gov/dig

A Note to Treasure Hunters

Treasure hunters are a unique breed. Most aren't willing to share information until they have exhausted their own efforts... and even then, it might be a while. Each bit of gathered information is a precious piece of the puzzle. We can relate!

Being treasure hunters ourselves, when we see news of treasure found, we are quick to spot what's "not" being said. That inside information that goes below the surface and would probably change the outlook of the whole event.

However, we also have another way of looking at things... by helping others, we also help ourselves. Believing that "doing good and helping others" comes back around in some way, maybe even coming from some other direction!

We do love treasure and all the possibilities that are in this book. However, if we are being honest (and we are), there are one or two specific pirate treasures in this book that we are highly interested in ourselves.

Which ones? We're not saying... lol!

Keep dreaming of treasure,
keep searching for treasure!

T&S Publications

T&S Publications

Hi Everyone,

  We are a brother and sister team (Thomas and Susan) with a shared passion for all kinds of treasure hunting (and treasure, of course).
  We love going on treasure hunting trips together and on our own as much as possible.
  In fact, the next big treasure always has our attention, such as the historic treasures in this book to current treasures like the lottery!
  We have enjoyed making this book! Thank you so much for including us in **your** passion for treasure! All the best!!

Sincerely,
T&S Publications

Pirates
and their Lost Treasures

An Informative Guide For Treasure Hunters!

by
T&S Publications

To visit us, put into your browser:
www.tspublications.net

For fun Treasure Hunting/Metal Detecting designs on tee-shirts and over 70 products, visit our store at: http://TreasureTime.redbubble.com

It's Treasure Time!

www.ingramcontent.com/pod-product-compliance
Lightning Source LLC
Chambersburg PA
CBHW062009070426
42451CB00008BA/304